FLOODS

By Jennifer Howse

www.av2books.com

AV² provides enriched content that supplements and complements this book. Weigl's AV² books strive to create inspired learning and engage young minds in a total learning experience.

Your AV² Media Enhanced books come alive with...

Audio
Listen to sections of the book read aloud.

Key Words
Study vocabulary, and complete a matching word activity.

Video
Watch informative video clips.

Quizzes
Test your knowledge.

Go to **www.av2books.com**, and enter this book's unique code.

Embedded Weblinks
Gain additional information for research.

Slide Show
View images and captions, and prepare a presentation.

BOOK CODE

E882435

AV² by Weigl brings you media enhanced books that support active learning.

Try This!
Complete activities and hands-on experiments.

... and much, much more!

Published by AV² by Weigl
350 5th Avenue, 59th Floor
New York, NY 10118
Websites: www.av2books.com   www.weigl.com

Library of Congress Control Number: 2014934640
ISBN 978-1-4896-1206-9 (hardcover)
ISBN 978-1-4896-1207-6 (softcover)
ISBN 978-1-4896-1208-3 (single-user eBook)
ISBN 978-1-4896-1209-0 (multi-user eBook)

Printed in the United States of America in North Mankato, Minnesota
1 2 3 4 5 6 7 8 9 0 18 17 16 15 14

052014
WEP090514

Senior Editor: Aaron Carr
Art Director: Terry Paulhus

Contents

Floods Are One of the Deadliest Natural Disasters in the World

A natural disaster is when sudden shifts in land and weather take place all at once to create extreme conditions. These conditions can cause widespread damage and endanger human and animal life. Natural disasters can also wipe out vegetation or forever change landscape of a region. In the case of flooding, the effects can be severe and long-lasting.

Flooding is a natural disaster that results from high water flow that rises too quickly to properly drain. Land is quickly **submerged** under water. The **ebb and flow** of water through river systems is a normal and predictable occurrence. Minor amounts of flooding are expected in river systems, such as the annual flooding the Amazon River in South America. The river can reach 50 miles (80 kilometers) wide during the flood season. The forest plants and animals have adapted to the seasonal flooding. The people who live near the river also adapt to the normal seasonal rise and fall of the Amazon River. However, if the amount of water is too much within a short period of time, that can lead to a disaster.

Extreme amounts of rainfall can cause lakes to overflow and flood the surrounding area.

Floods in major cities can lead to closed roads that may take weeks or even months to drain and reopen.

Most Floods Are Caused by Too Much Rain

Floods can happen anywhere there is a body of water, such as a river, lake, or ocean. The amount of flooding, or how often flooding happens, depends on different conditions. Most flooding is caused by too much rain. Water **evaporates** into the **atmosphere** from the surface of Earth. The water collects in clouds and then falls back to Earth as **precipitation**. This process is called the water cycle.

People who live in areas at high risk of flooding often build **levees** to hold back rising flood waters.

Water settles in pools, ponds, lakes, and rivers. This is called surface water. Some of the water is **absorbed** into the ground. Any water that is not absorbed into the soil flows downhill toward low areas. These areas are called **basins**. Flooding is the result of too much water in stream and river channels. The soil cannot absorb any more water, so the water rises above the channel's edge and flows out over the **flood plain**.

Floods often overflow sewage systems, causing water to pour out of sewer drains.

Natural Causes

TOO MUCH precipitation over an area within a short period of time

Spring thaw happening too fast due to sudden warm weather

Hurricanes or Tsunamis breaking waves on shorelines

VS

Human Causes

CLEAR CUTTING of trees which removes vital root systems along river shorelines

Erosion due to farming, which removes important top soil

Floods Can Sometimes Be Controlled

Monitoring areas where floods can happen is important. It is also challenging because flooding can happen anywhere in the world. Scientists keep track of long-term weather patterns and the movement of water over land. Understanding these normal patterns of water levels and water flow is vital because flood conditions can quickly build into a natural disaster if early warning systems are not in place.

Floods can sometimes be **mitigated**. This means that, with careful monitoring and planning, floods can be controlled and the damage decreased. Controlling floods depends on taking regular measurements of water levels and the water flow speeds. Making waterway maps is also important. These maps show how water **runoff** flows and pools in certain areas.

Water level indicators show the height of flood waters.

Planning for floods includes reviewing the amount of risk involved in building or living close to waterways. This review takes into account how much rain will likely fall within a year and how much time will pass between flood events. In 1930, the United States government began a project to control the flooding of the Mississippi River. Monitoring systems were put in place. Another system to control the flow of water was also created. Many reservoirs, three hundred **dams**, and thousands of miles (km) of levees were also built.

Levees cannot always keep out all of the water from a flood. For severe or long-lasting floods, water often has to be pumped out of the area inside the levee.

People fill bags with sand and pile them to make walls to keep out flood water. Sandbag walls are often built around houses and other buildings.

Wetlands Can Prevent Floods

Natural **wetland**s that lie along waterways are one of the best ways to prevent flooding. A wetland may be called a bog, a swamp, a fen, or a marsh. Wetlands act like sponges, absorbing extra water and increasing the amount of water that the river system can hold. They hold this extra water and slowly release it back into the river system. This cycle is the best prevention for flooding.

Water basins are areas where water drains into wetlands and traps excess water at the important headwaters of rivers. Water is either evaporated directly into the atmosphere, or it is released slowly into runoff streams, which also prevent waterways from drying out.

Each year, about 2.6 cubic miles (11 cubic kilometers) of water spreads over the 6,500 square miles (16,800 square kilometers) area of the Okavango Delta in Botswana, Africa.

People often destroy wetlands to build houses and other buildings along riverways. These areas offer access to fresh water, fertile land, and a transportation route for boats. However, this can cause problems when too many wetlands are developed. Removing these wetlands also removes the natural flood protection that wetlands provide. One way to prevent floods is to make more wetlands in areas that are known to flood. Scientists must be careful when choosing where to put a human-made wetland. The chosen place must allow for water to flow naturally, and it must reduce the chance of flooding in the future. However, human-made wetlands often do not prevent floods as well as natural wetlands do.

Flooding can damage farmers' crops and destroy entire harvests. Sometimes, the floods carry away important nutrients in the soil. This makes it harder for the land to support new crops later.

50 IN 5

Flash floods have happened in all 50 American states in the past five years.

Just 2 feet (0.6 m) of water can wash a car away.

The peat found in many wetlands is up to 98% water.

FLASH FLOOD

A flash flood can cause a **wall of water** 20 feet (6 meters) high.

All-Time Records

Humans have lived along waterways for thousands of years. Understanding the patterns of the natural ebb and flow of water is a matter of survival. Terrible floods have taken place in most parts of the world. These floods have often caught people unprepared, resulting in huge losses of life and destruction of landscapes.

DEADLIEST

In 1931, China's Yellow River breached it banks and drowned as many as four million people. **Silt** is carried down this river. The silt builds up on the river bottom until the river is higher than its banks. This is how the Yellow River flooded in 1931. Today, levees are used to try to keep the river from overflowing its banks.

STRONGEST

The Netherlands has some of the world's most advanced flood control systems. This is due to a long history of flooding. The Great Storm of 1287 broke a dike. As many as 80,000 people died. Historical records also show that this storm formed in the English Channel and caused damage and deaths in Great Britain.

MOST DAMAGE

The Mississippi River flooded in 1993. Many people live along this river. Many of the levees, **flood walls**, and dams in place to protect these people failed. Areas affected by the flood included 11 states. Entire towns were lost to water damage, and growing areas were wiped out. Total damages from the flood were estimated at $20 billion.

FASTEST

The Johnstown, Pennsylvania, flood of 1889 was the result of a dam burst. The spring thaw was happening quickly, sending water rushing down the Conemaugh and the Stony Creek Rivers. When part of the dam failed, it released a wall of water reaching up 40 feet (12 meters) tall and half a mile (0.8 km) wide. The 20 million tons (18 million metric tons) of water roared through Johnstown and left 2,209 people dead.

Flooding in the United States

Flooding has occurred in every state in the United States of America. This is the most common type of natural disaster. Over the past 30 years, an average of 89 people per year died in flash floods. Of these deaths, more than 60 percent were people caught in their vehicles and swept away with the water. There is also millions of dollars in damage each year to buildings, streets, and other structures.

Washington

Oregon

Idaho

Montana

Wyoming

Nevada

Utah

Colorado

California

Arizona

New Mexico

Pacific Ocean

SPRING FLOOD RISK

HIGH RISK

MODERATE RISK

LOW RISK

MAP SCALE

0   500 mi

500 km

North Dakota

Minnesota

South Dakota

Wisconsin

Michigan

New Hampshire

Vermont

Maine

Massachusetts

New York

Rhode Island

Pennsylvania

Connecticut

New Jersey

Delaware

Maryland

Nebraska

Iowa

Illinois

Indiana

Ohio

West Virginia

Virginia

Kansas

Missouri

Kentucky

Oklahoma

Tennessee

North Carolina

Arkansas

South Carolina

Texas

Mississippi

Alabama

Georgia

Atlantic Ocean

Louisiana

Florida

Gulf of Mexico

Bangladesh Is One of the Most Flooded Countries in the World

Bangladesh is one of most flooded countries in the world. Most of the land mass of Bangladesh is flood plains. The Ganges and the Brahmaputra are the two rivers that run through the region. These rivers are normally about 10 miles (16 km) wide, but during the rainy monsoon season the rivers can grow up to 100 miles (160 km) across.

An increase in development on flood plains has greatly increased the number of floods in Bangladesh.

The region is prone to flooding because most of the country is only 16 feet (5 m) above sea level. The natural annual flooding is part of the agricultural cycle that deposits rich soil used by farmers to grow rice and other crops. However, flooding is becoming more extreme. It is causing more damage and resulting in more deaths. Development in the nearby countries of Nepal and India is having an effect on the flooding in Bangladesh. Floods are growing in size due to loss of trees through **deforestation** in Nepal and because of dams built in India.

During a monsoon, it is not unusual for as much as 20 percent of the country to become flooded.

The Flood of
1998
Bangladesh

Two-thirds of the country was submerged for more than three months.

30 million people were affected

10,000 miles of roads, 14,000 school buildings and 500,000 homes were damaged

1,000 people died

American Scientist Robert E. Horton created the Horton Overflow

The study of hydrology is the study of water. This study involves understanding how water flows, how it is distributed, and how it is evaporated. A hydrologist researches the water cycle. This is the process by which water is constantly recycled.

Robert E. Horton was scientist who studied how water drained from streams. After studying the flow of water through streams, Horton used math to measure how much water flowed into a drainage system and how fast it moved. He created a math formula called the Horton's Infiltration Equation. This formula measures infiltration, or the seepage of water into the soil. He also studied soil erosion and how erosion can change the land and how that can change how the water runoff flows.

After Hurricane Sandy, hydrologists retrieved more than 150 storm-surge sensors. These sensors were placed just before the hurricane made landfall. They provided hydrologists with important information regarding the water levels that led to extensive flooding

One of Horton's inventions is the water level gauge. A scale is mounted above the water. A chain is attached to the scale at one end and a weight, called a plumb-bob, at the other end. The plumb-bob sinks to the bottom, and the depth is shown on the scale at the surface.

Today, hydrologists continue to use their understanding of math and science to try to gain a better understanding of the water cycle. They use equipment to collect information they can use to help plan for, prevent, or control flooding. Hydrologists create models that predict the possibility of flooding. These scientists may work in urban planning and water management. They may also work in environmental protection to prevent water pollution.

Gauging stations are locations where water gauges are placed. They provide hydrologists with continuous records of a particular location's water levels. The data collected at these stations provides hydrologists with the information they need to make their predictions.

Little Known Facts

100 YEAR FLOOD

Predicting the possibility of a flood happening in a region is done with a classification system. Scientists collect data and determine how likely a flood will be within a period of time. A 100 year flood is a large flood that may only happen once every 100 years. This means that there is only a one percent chance that a flood of that size will happen within one year.

URBANIZATION

Cities are often built near waterways. The concrete streets and buildings do not allow the natural ebb and flow of water. **Storm drains** are designed to let only a set amount of water through. Too much rain can make the system fail. If there is more rain than the drainage system can handle, floods will happen.

JÖKULHLAUP

Jökulhlaup is a term from Iceland that refers to lakes that are dammed by huge pieces of ice. Water can seep through these blocks of ice. This melts the ice. More and more water fills the lake until the pressure from the water breaks up the big chunks of ice. A flash flood then sends water rushing above the shoreline of the lake.

FROZEN SOIL

In northern areas, too much precipitation during winter can lead to flood conditions. If the ground is frozen, soil cannot absorb runoff water as well. Scientists take measurements on the amount of frost in the ground, the amount of snow cover, the temperature, and how much water is entering the soil. By putting all of these measurements together, they can create of a model of possible flood conditions.

WINDY WEATHER

Gale force winds can create flood conditions. Extreme wind speeds across the surface of a body of water, such as a sea or large lake, can whip up water and send it crashing along the shoreline. The extreme winds can also affect the Earth's atmosphere by stirring up weather systems to create huge rain clouds.

People Have Come Up With Many Ways to Try to Prevent Floods

As people develop more and more land near waterways, there is a greater need for flood control. A country that has many systems of flood control is the Netherlands. About half of the land area of the Netherlands is less than 3 feet (1 m) above the sea level. Destructive floods in the 12th century caused the Dutch to come up with new ways of controlling water. One of these new water control methods was a system of **windmills**. Tall mills with four sails capture the wind, causing the sails to rotate. The power from the rotating sails is used to turn an **Archimedes' screw**. This screw carries water from one place to another. In this way, windmills helped control how much water settled on the land.

The oldest mill in the Netherlands is a water mill that dates back to the eighth century.

In the 19th century, steam was used to power large pumping stations. These stations pumped water out of one area and into another. Today, the Netherlands has some of the world's most advanced water drainage systems. This is necessary because about two-thirds of the country is threatened by flooding. Engineers there are looking at nature to help them make better water control systems. They use natural materials and attempt to copy natural systems. The aim is to make room for extra water flow so that it will not lead to flooding. Levees, dams, drainage ditches, floodplains, and canals form a complex network of flood control systems that span the country.

In the past, levees were made from natural materials, such as wood, sand, and clay. A protective clay outer layer was placed on top of a core of sand. The clay helped keep the levee from eroding.

Floods Cause Billions of Dollars in Damage

Flood conditions can arise very quickly when a dam bursts or a levee fails. Floods can also take place slowly, with huge amounts of water moving downstream with no way to stop the flow. Though each flood is different, the damage floods create is very much the same. In the United States, the National Oceanic Atmospheric Administration (NOAA) watches for signs of flooding. The NOAA informs local emergency services when a flood may happen. People may be asked to stay inside. In the event of severe flooding, people may be evacuated to higher ground.

Floodwaters cause widespread damage. The force of the rushing water destroys homes and businesses. Mold sets into wooden buildings. Even metal and concrete structures, such as bridges and high-rise buildings, may collapse under the force of the water.

Floodwaters that are just 2 feet (0.6 m) in height are powerful enough to carry away a car.

People living in flooded areas can be left without power and clean drinking water for days, weeks, or even months after the flood. This may lead to outbreaks of diseases such typhoid, hepatitis A, and cholera. Even after the floodwaters are gone, tons (metric tons) of silt, sand, and other types of debris are left behind. The cleanup after a flood may take years to complete and cost billions of dollars.

OTHER TYPES OF DISASTERS

Earthquakes

The shifting of the Earth's tectonic plates causes Earth's surface to rumble and shake. This shifting can smash large pieces of land together so it rises up or separates. Earthquakes can cause a great deal of damage to buildings and other structures. They can also cause other disasters, such as landslides, floods, or tsunamis.

Tornado

A rotating thunderstorm creates the conditions needed for a tornado to touch down to the ground. Scientists cannot fully explain why tornados develop. A funnel cloud forms and spins around a calm center. This funnel cloud moves with enough force to rip apart buildings and landscapes in an instant.

Landslide

Erosion due to rainfall, or practices such as mining, can cause landslides. The land on a slope becomes too heavy or loose for the ground to hold. Gravity then pulls the land down the slope. Landslides are sudden and quick events that are dangerous because boulders, mud, and debris rush downhill at high speeds. This is why landslides are one of the deadliest natural disasters.

The Great Flood and Emperor Yu

A country with a long history of terrible flooding events is China. Several flood stories are part of Chinese mythology and they center on controlling the flood waters. As early as 4,000 BC, the Chinese Miao people have shared a story. It tells of a great flood and how only two people survived. In the story, a god named Ziene and another god named Thunder try to destroy the Earth with too much rain. The Miao people did not have any form of writing in their language. Instead, they told memorable stories to share knowledge or record important events.

THE GREAT FLOOD OF CHINA (2205 BC)

Heavy rains fell, and the countryside was filling with water that had no escape. Emperor Yao went to his advisors, the four mountains, for advice on how to stop the flooding. The mountains told the Emperor to hire his cousin Gun to stop the flooding. Gun was hired and took expanding soil from a god. He used the soil to build dams and barriers, but all of this failed to control the floods. After nine years of failure, another Emperor, called Shun, came to help. After several more years, the floods could not be controlled. Gun lost his job, which was given to his son Yu. Yu made drainage systems to reduced the floods. Water was directed to run into the nine great rivers and out to sea. Emperor Shun was so grateful to Yu that he gave him the crown instead of Shun's own son. Now, he is remembered at the Great Emperor Yu.

Flood Timeline

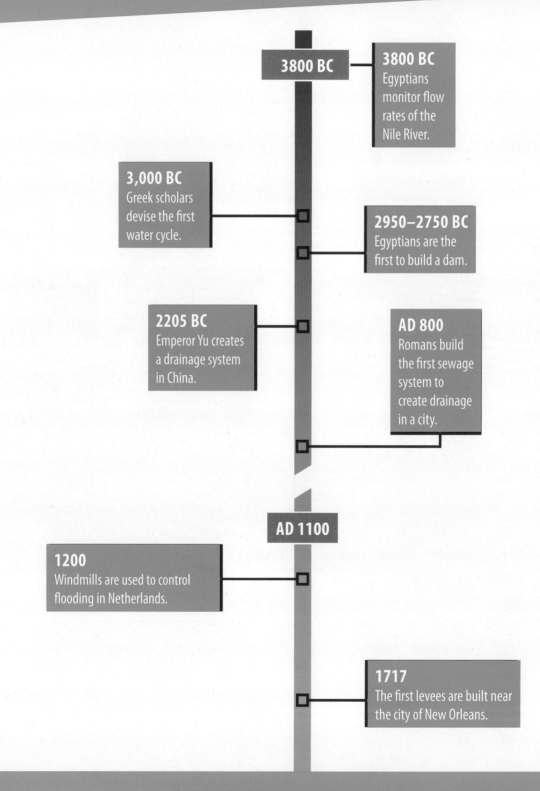

3800 BC

3800 BC
Egyptians monitor flow rates of the Nile River.

3,000 BC
Greek scholars devise the first water cycle.

2950–2750 BC
Egyptians are the first to build a dam.

2205 BC
Emperor Yu creates a drainage system in China.

AD 800
Romans build the first sewage system to create drainage in a city.

AD 1100

1200
Windmills are used to control flooding in Netherlands.

1717
The first levees are built near the city of New Orleans.

Test Your Knowledge

1 What is the process that constantly recycles water on Earth?

A. The water cycle

2 How does a wind mill move water?

A. With an Archimedes' screw

3 What is the name of the barriers built along the Mississippi River?

A. Levees

4 What weather condition causes most floods?

A. Too much rain in a short period of time

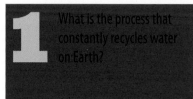

5 List two reasons why Bangladesh floods more than any other country?

A. Deforestation and dam building

6 Which country has the most advanced flood control systems in the world?

A. The Netherlands

7 What is a water basin?

A. Where runoff water naturally is stored and is slowly released

8 What river in China has caused many deadly floods, including the deadliest flood ever recorded?

A. The Yellow River

9 What are some diseases that can be spread by dirty or standing water during flood events?

A. Typhoid, Hepatitis A, and Cholera

10 What did Yu build to stop flooding in the tale The Great Flood of China?

A. Drainage systems

Hydrology Monitoring

O ne of the best ways to prevent flood damage is to watch water levels. Hydrologists consider two things when they take measurements. The first is the volume of water, and the second is the length of time it took the water to reach that level. Precipitation can be tracked by building your own water level measurement tool.

1 Take the ruler and the plastic container and black marker. Using the ruler, mark a line on the container every 1/4 of an inch (5 millimeters). Note that the bottom of the container is zero.

2 Make a graph. On the bottom of the graph, put increments of the time from 0 to 24 hours. The left side of the graph is volume of water from 0 to 1 inch (0 to 25 mm).

3 Wait for a rainy day or snowfall. Place the plastic container outside to collect the precipitation. Plan to check the water level once an hour (except when you are sleeping), and plot the volume of water at each time on the graph.

4 Draw a line along the plot points on your graph. Did you observe a large amount of rainfall? If you collected snow, did it melt? How much water was left? How much more precipitation would it have taken to overflow your container?

What You Need
- What you need
- Clear plastic container that can hold at least 0.7 ounces (20 milliliters) of liquid
- Black permanent marker
- Paper and pencil
- Ruler

Key Words

absorbed: to soak up

Archimedes' screw: a large screw that moves water from one place to another

atmosphere: the layer of air and other gases that surrounds the Earth

basins: areas in which water from runoff pools and is slowly released back into rivers

dams: structures that block the flow of water

deforestation: clearing an area of all forests or trees

ebb and flow: regular movement of water, often related to tides

evaporates: turns from liquid to vapor, as in the change from water to steam

flood plain: the natural lowlands where overflow water settles

flood walls: large walls that redirect water away from an urban area

levees: mounds of earth along waterways to prevent overflow

mitigated: made less destructive or deadly

precipitation: water in the form of rain, snow, or hail that falls from the upper atmosphere

runoff: rain or snowmelt that flows toward large bodies of water

silt: fine sand or clay carried in rivers and floodwaters

storm drains: human-made systems for emptying urban areas of excess water

submerged: put completely underwater

wetlands: areas in which excess water is filtered and held

windmills: wind-powered mills that remove excess water from the land

Index

Log on to www.av2books.com

AV² by Weigl brings you media enhanced books that support active learning. Go to www.av2books.com, and enter the special code found on page 2 of this book. You will gain access to enriched and enhanced content that supplements and complements this book. Content includes video, audio, weblinks, quizzes, a slide show, and activities.

AV² Online Navigation

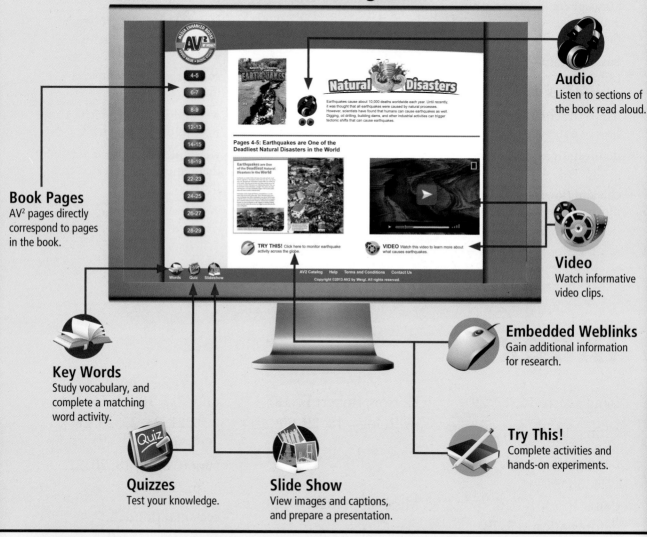

Audio
Listen to sections of the book read aloud.

Video
Watch informative video clips.

Book Pages
AV² pages directly correspond to pages in the book.

Key Words
Study vocabulary, and complete a matching word activity.

Quizzes
Test your knowledge.

Slide Show
View images and captions, and prepare a presentation.

Embedded Weblinks
Gain additional information for research.

Try This!
Complete activities and hands-on experiments.

AV² was built to bridge the gap between print and digital. We encourage you to tell us what you like and what you want to see in the future.

Sign up to be an AV² Ambassador at www.av2books.com/ambassador.